Tony the Tripod Tiger

Adventures of a Three-legged Tiger Cub

Michael Peter Wilson

Tellwell Talent
www.tellwell.ca

ISBN
978-0-2288-4624-6 (Hardcover)
978-0-2288-4623-9 (Paperback)

Introduction

Imagine a land of high mountains and jungle covered in lush plants with leaves as big as elephant ears. This is a land where cats grow larger than people and they watch from up in the trees.

This land is called India, where beautiful animals like Bengal tigers, black panthers, striped hyenas, and colourful peacocks roam free.

These rare animals hide when people arrive, but if you're very quiet and let your imagination go free, nobody knows what magic you'll see.

Tony likes to hide and jump and play all day. The jungle is full of surprises but Momma is never far away. He chases a bug with a smile and a grin. He's wandered too far, and big trouble he's in.

Oh No! Oh My!

Ella, a rare black panther, hears Tony's cry and thinks, *Oh No! Oh My! My babies are gone but that one is alive.* She slinks close through the grass, being careful to hide. She waits for his momma to come back by his side.

Henny the Hyena perks up her ears; she laughs and she barks at the sound of fear. She is jealous of tigers so revered and bright as they look down on all others from their lofty height. As she emerges out of the scrub, now is her chance to make fun of this cub.

Now is my chance to get my name out of the mud.

Help me, Momma; wait up
for me, please!

Henny's barking and laughter make Tony jump; he leaps
and he lands with barely a bump. Nothing can stop him;
his heartbeats thump-thump.

Tony escapes as he jumps from the barks, and Henny disappears into the dark. Tony leaps to a branch but he misses the mark.

Tony fell far to the ground. He has broken his leg, bonked his head hard, and fallen asleep. Little Tony is hurt badly; he is very weak. Without Momma's help, his future is bleak.

Jordan the Peacock is up on a vine; strutting high in the sky is his favourite pastime. He hears Henny's barks and sees Tony fly by. When the little cub hits the ground, there is a most terrible sound.

Oh, poor little tiger! I'll make sure help comes around.

Jordan swoops down to the cub on the ground. Oh, what a terrible scene he has found. He spreads out his tail feathers and makes the brightest display. Ella sees Jordan and runs over that way.

Come quickly, Miss Ella; we must take him away.

We need a doctor!
We need a vet!

Ella picks up Tony by the scruff of his neck. They need to find soon any help they can get. The little cub is a wreck; they must get Tony to the tiger vet!

Jordan leads, in a colourful display, calling out for help every step of the way.

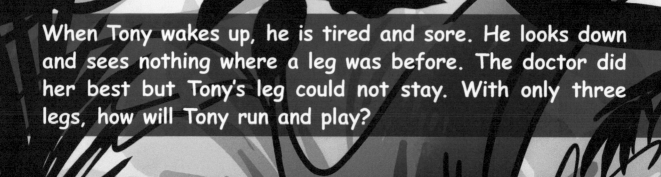

When Tony wakes up, he is tired and sore. He looks down and sees nothing where a leg was before. The doctor did her best but Tony's leg could not stay. With only three legs, how will Tony run and play?

The doctor decided that three legs was best. Now lay down your worried head and rest. You will learn to play in a different way. Tomorrow will be a better day.

1 2 3... where is the rest of me? 1 2 3... why did this happen to me?

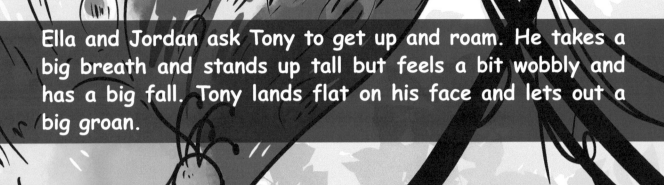

Ella and Jordan ask Tony to get up and roam. He takes a big breath and stands up tall but feels a bit wobbly and has a big fall. Tony lands flat on his face and lets out a big groan.

1 2 3... Don't count what you see. Take a deep breath, stand up, and just be. Four legs were for a different type of race. Although it is true you may stumble and fall, just take a deep breath and stand up tall.

1 2 3... look and see! How can I be when I'm missing part of me?

Grrrooan!

Run, Tony, run; you are fast and strong! Believe in yourself and you'll never go wrong.

I can hop and jump and run really fast; look at me sneak and skulk through the long grass.

It doesn't take long for Tony to heal. He walks with a hop and a skip and a jump. He even leaps over big rocks and tree stumps. When Tony stumbles or falls on his face, his friends remind him to take a new pace.

Ella remembers her babies long gone and takes care of little Tony like one of her own. She licks and licks to keep Tony clean, giving his stripes a beautiful sheen. It feels like a dream being loved, being cleaned, Tony feels so happy that he kicks and he screams.

Lick Lick Lick

Kick Kick Kick

Tony is happy to have his new friends but he misses his mom and wonders what happened that day. His mom was brave and protected her cub. Where is she now when he longs for her love?

Where is my momma?
Why didn't she stay?

Your momma saw the hyena hunt you that day. She loved you so much she chased it away

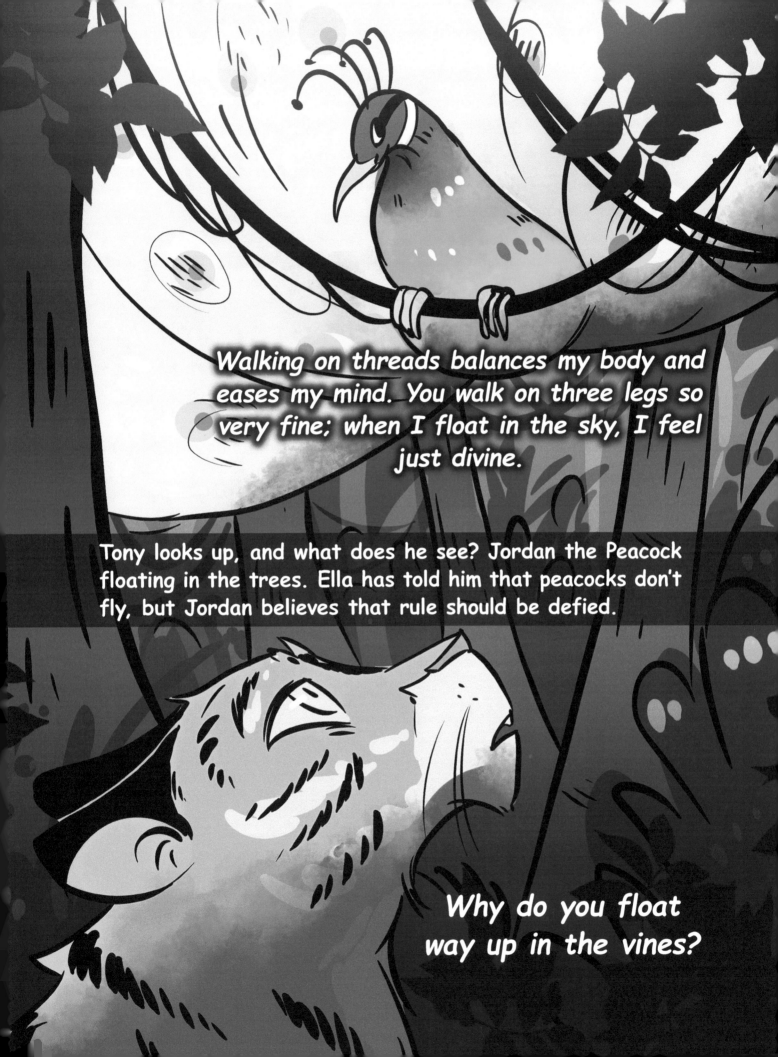

Walking on threads balances my body and eases my mind. You walk on three legs so very fine; when I float in the sky, I feel just divine.

Tony looks up, and what does he see? Jordan the Peacock floating in the trees. Ella has told him that peacocks don't fly, but Jordan believes that rule should be defied.

Why do you float way up in the vines?

Henny is back, watching Tony play, waiting for a chance when he can't get away. That silly peacock with his outlandish displays and an old momma panther won't keep her at bay.

Ha Ha Ha Ha! Bark Bark Bark! Just you wait until it gets dark!

Tony likes to sleep in a cave in the rocks. He feels safe from the night and the sounds in the dark. Henny followed the cub where he walked; now she waits at the entrance, licking her chops.

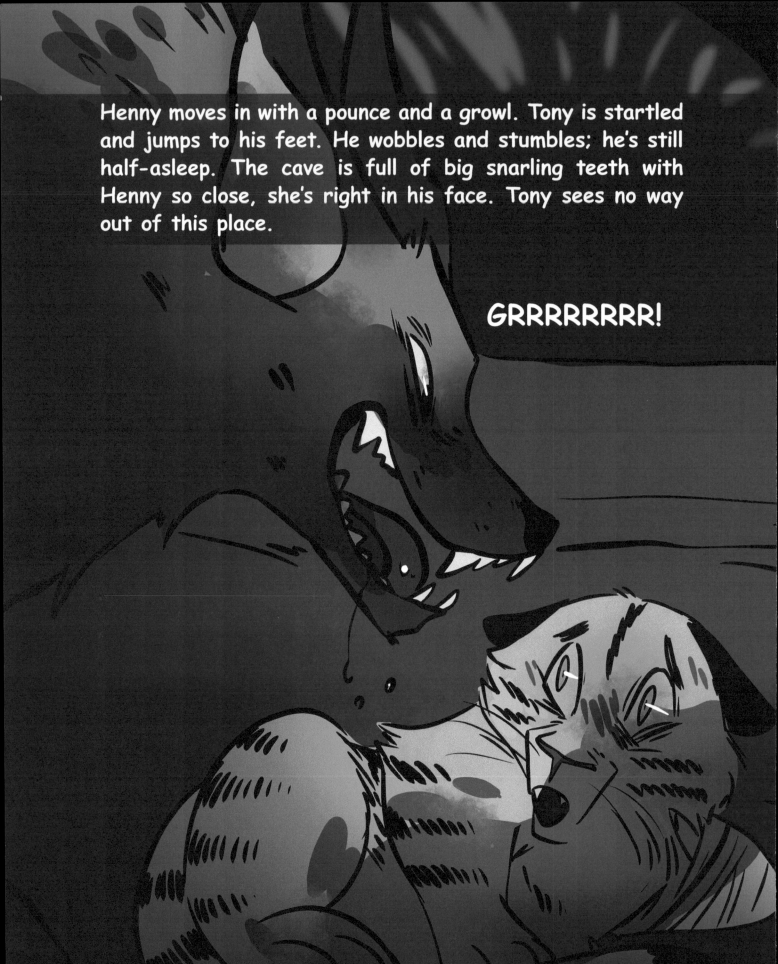

Henny moves in with a pounce and a growl. Tony is startled and jumps to his feet. He wobbles and stumbles; he's still half-asleep. The cave is full of big snarling teeth with Henny so close, she's right in his face. Tony sees no way out of this place.

GRRRRRRRR!

ROOOAAAAAAR!!!

Tony's heart beats so fast he feels like he's frozen but he stands up tall, takes a big breath, and puffs up his chest. He must face this beast or it will be certain death. Tony lets out a roar so loud and long, it fills the whole jungle like an echoing song.

Henny runs faster than any hyena before. Tony stands tall and tells her no more. Henny still envies Tony's beautiful stripes and loud roar, but she never returns to settle the score.

1 2 3... Look and see, Tony the tripod tiger, happy and free.

Tony learned on that day what it is to be brave. He just needed to breathe, believe and stand on all threes. As he grew, Ella taught him the secrets of big cat life: how to sneak through tall grass and watch over the jungle up in the trees.

When Tony felt lonely or didn't feel strong, he looked up in the sky to see Jordan floating on vines and that made him smile all the day long.